"In this crisp, clear and brightly written introduction to Christianity, Glen shows how we are made to receive gifts and why that turns out to be wonderful news when we encounter the Giver."

Andrew Wilson, Teaching Pastor, King's Church London

"Glen Scrivener has written a fascinating and compelling guide to the Gift behind our Christmas gifts. It was refreshing for me as a long-time Christian but will also be one of the first things I give to someone who might want to think about this for the very first time."

Sam Allberry, Speaker and Author

"The gospel is wrapped up in Glen's humble and winsome words. He shows us how our give-and-take Christmas traditions can point us to the gracious Giver. This is worth sharing with family and friends!"

Quina Aragon, Author, *Love Made: A Story of God's Overflowing, Creative Heart*

"Accessible, encouraging and inspiring. This powerful book is a must-read for anyone exploring the real meaning of Christmas."

Gavin Calver, Director of Mission, Evangelical Alliance

"Christmas is a fantastic time to point people to Jesus, God's greatest gift. In this easy-to-give-away book Glen uses his gifts as a wordsmith and communicator to do just that."

Roy Crowne, Executive Director, HOPE

"*The Gift* is a wonderful reflection on the act of giving presents. It starts with experiences we all share and uses these to explore what it means to be human, what it means to love and be loved, what it means to connect with the self-giving Love at the heart of reality, with God. It all adds up to a delightful book to read and a great present to give."

Tim Chester, Pastor, Grace Church Boroughbridge;
Faculty Member of Crosslands Training

GLEN SCRIVENER

THE GIFT

thegoodbook
COMPANY

The Gift
© Glen Scrivener 2019

Published by:
The Good Book Company

thegoodbook.com | www.thegoodbook.co.uk
thegoodbook.com.au | thegoodbook.co.nz | thegoodbook.co.in

ISBN: 9781784983741 | Printed in India

Design by André Parker

CONTENTS

INTRODUCTION

"You shouldn't have!"

"I couldn't help myself."

"It's far too much!"

"I had to. It's you all over."

"It's perfect!"

"I knew you'd like it."

"I LOVE it!"

Giving and receiving is the heart of Christmas. It's the heart of life, really, but on one day in particular we wrap it up in paper and tie a bow on top. It becomes a dance which we teach our children from their earliest days: "Wait your turn!" "Give Lily her present!" "Say thank you!" "Card first!" "Give Auntie Joan a kiss!" "Don't cry; socks are *very thoughtful!*"

Whether or not we think of ourselves as traditional, we all tend to be stuck in our ways when it comes to Christmas. You may imagine yourself to be reasonable, modern and completely happy-go-lucky, but all of us fall into patterns, year after year. We probably don't notice them until there's a stranger in our midst—our sister's new boyfriend, perhaps, or some exchange student who can't get home for the holidays. It's not long before we discover an inner voice rising up: "Oh dear, poor soul... They're Getting Christmas Wrong." Without doubt, they are thinking the exact same thing of us.

Perhaps you have been that stranger in someone else's Christmas. I have been, many times. Everyone else seems to know the rules. It's all second nature to them—but you're left gawking at the action from the sofa, as if you're watching the first episode of a Scandinavian crime drama: *"How's he related to her again? Is this normal where they're from? What's happening now? Shall I Google it?"*

You try to smile your way through the day, making sure to compliment the cook at least 17 times on their prawn cocktail. It can be exhausting. But none of the insiders think it's strange. No, no. It's all just The Way Christmas Happens Around Here.

But I wonder how a true outsider would find our Christmases. What would an alien make of our gift-giving, for instance? It's all so odd. We go to extraordinary lengths to keep the gifts secret. We hide the receipts, we hide the shopping bags, we hide the purchases under beds and on top of wardrobes. We conceal the presents in special coloured paper (whole multi-million dollar industries are founded on this one peculiarity!). Before we reveal the gifts, we haul a tree inside—a six-foot Norwegian pine tree plonked in the middle of the living room (or, stranger still, a *plastic imitation* of a six-foot Norwegian pine tree)—just so that we can arrange the gifts underneath.

Then, finally, the wait is over, and Christmas Day arrives. The presents are exchanged.

Everyone has their own traditions for this part too. Some families have a grab-and-rip free-for-all. Others are more orderly, as each person around the circle receives the gift, weighs it, shakes it and dutifully exclaims, "I wonder what this could be!" It's all a pantomime. It's all ridiculous. But we love it, so we do it anyway.

For most of us, Christmas morning is a time-honoured gift-giving ritual where each move is important. We know our parts. We play our roles. We might make fun of our peculiar traditions, but we have those traditions for a reason: giving and receiving is serious business.

Ever wondered why?

Giving

Bring to mind the moment on Christmas morning when you hand over a well-considered present. Not an Amazon gift card. Not a box of chocolates. Something meaningful. Perhaps something far too expensive, or something handmade, or something you saw back in April and you just knew this was it. Now is the moment. You hand it to your loved one, and they reach out to take it. In between you exists the gift. It's more than a purchase cloaked in green paper and sticky tape. In that moment, the gift handed over is *you*.

When it comes to important presents, we put *ourselves* into them. They are not just things: they communicate *us*, and how much the other person means to us. And when a gift is received with joy and gratitude, there is no better feeling in the world. We're ecstatic. And I mean that literally, because that word "ecstatic" comes from the Greek for "standing outside yourself". The whole flow of give-and-take is about handing yourself over to someone you love in the form of that gift. You put your heart and soul into the present and when it's received, in a deep sense you are being received. Through the present you've gone beyond yourself and have found a home in someone else's embrace. You are "beside yourself". Giving is ecstasy.

Receiving

Now think of receiving a gift. Again, not a gift card but something precious. Perhaps you've had your eye on it for ages but you haven't allowed yourself to hope for something so expensive. Or perhaps this particular present never crossed your mind—you didn't even know it existed. But as soon as you see it, you know it's right. Instinctively you cry out, "Wow, it's perfect! You didn't have to!" At that point the giver will smile and say, "I know I didn't have to. I wanted to!" And they mean it, too. It was a pleasure to give—ecstasy even.

Most often, receiving gifts is just part of the Christmas rigmarole. We tear off the paper and enthuse: "Oh! Soap on a rope! Again! You really shouldn't have!" And only the last part of that response is properly heartfelt. But then, once in a blue moon, there are gifts that truly touch us—

gifts that really are "far too much". They're an experience of grace, of getting more than we could possibly deserve. To be on the receiving end of this kind of generosity is to be seen, known and valued over and above all expectations. As we receive it, we are touched not just by the value of the gift but by the valuation of the giver. They really shouldn't have. But they wanted to. Because they wanted us. They wanted to show that they love us. The experience is thrilling.

That's what makes Christmas (or at least, the idea of Christmas) such a welcome break from the rest of our lives. For the most part, our lives are about striving. We spend our lives earning respect, earning status, earning our place. We chase rewards and success and payments. But even if we obtain them, at best they make us feel proud, or necessary, or just plain exhausted. They cannot give us what we most crave: we want to be wanted—to be loved.

That's why the give-and-take of Christmas means so much to us. That's why we protect the traditions and wrap up the presents and bring in the tree. Because giving and receiving is what we were made for.

1. "IT'S FOR YOU"

Not all gifts come wrapped in paper. In fact, to be alive is to be in receipt of the most extraordinary gift imaginable.

"Life is a gift" might sound like a cliché—the kind of thing your auntie posts to Facebook. But it's true nonetheless. Think about it: we didn't have to exist. Before we existed, we were nobodies, made of nothing, living nowhere, and now… we have ourselves, we have a universe, we have everything. Utterly free. Utterly fantastic.

Life as a Gift

Do you ever think of your life as a gift? Consider this: we find ourselves living in a world that is humming with life and brimming with beauty. It's fascinating at every level of analysis, from the

Horsehead Nebula in outer space to the genetic code inside your cells. If this world was art, you'd call it magnificent. And, incredibly, you have a free lifetime pass to the gallery.

The world's magnificence comes at us through its cycles of seasons and sunsets—summer and winter, morning and evening—all offering their own distinct beauty. Each turn of the planet is more than a daily grind. It's graced with grandeur.

And the magnificence keeps coming, irrepressibly, through sights, sensations, flavours and sounds. Just think about music. There are harmonies and melodies so sublime that—whether it's Mozart or Miles Davis or Meat Loaf—we get carried away. Where? Somewhere beyond ourselves. Above the grind. Lost in the grandeur. It's that kind of a world.

Yes, the world is mangled too—there's darkness and death all around, for sure. We'll think more about that later. But it's a mangled *magnificence*. Whatever else might have taken up residence here on Planet Earth, this world also contains beauty, bliss and bumblebees. I know, *bumblebees*! Amazing! "You really didn't have to!" This world is a gift.

And then think of the you that's thinking about the world. You have a you-ness—a you-ness that is different from the world around you. A you-ness that is different from everyone else's you-ness. You didn't cause yourself to be conscious. You just found yourself in this reality machine—no charge, no fee. A gift.

Now let's personalise this. Think of your particular strengths, your talents, your... well, gifts. There are things you are able to do that are just fantastic. Genuinely. And they're unique to you. Where did those abilities come from? We call them "gifts" for a reason: we didn't give them to ourselves. But somewhere deep inside us a voice pipes up, "I've worked hard to get where I am today." And that's true too. But let's be honest. If you or I had been born in a village in the 9th century, would those talents and work ethic have earned us anything comparable to what we now claim as ours?

Which makes us consider the gift of our culture around us. The health, wealth, technology and freedoms which we enjoy today would have been unimaginable to our great-grandparents. And the society which makes them all possible is founded on certain "givens"—values that we just take for granted. It's a given that we should live under "the rule of law"—the principle that no particular person, government, business or interest group is above the law. All must play by the rules. Which rules? They're a given.

It's a given that we possess "human rights" that cannot be violated. We didn't have to think this way. After all, each person's chemical make-up is worth about as much as a Big Mac. Yet we value each person—no matter how poor, no matter how weak—far beyond their material properties or economic value. And we value each member of our society as the same—CEOs and street-sweepers are all equal. That's the ideal we prize, even if we don't always live it out. Such convictions lie at the heart of our culture, and yet we cannot prove them logically, mathematically or scientifically. To live in a society like ours, we simply have to rely on a whole raft of givens.

It's tempting, of course, to think that we humans have made our own way in the world. We have built the prosperity that we now enjoy through centuries of scientific discovery and technological advance. There is truth to this. But then, consider all the things that science and technology rely on. Why can we trust our senses, or the reliability of the laws of nature? Why do we have such a rationally ordered, scientifically explainable universe? Actually, we have to take it all as given.

And consider our brains—the ones doing all this considering. Perhaps, as with all animals, our brains help us survive and reproduce—but why then should we treat them as anything even approaching dependable when it comes to contemplating the higher laws of logic or the deeper mysteries of the cosmos? Yet we do. We humans take our own rational powers seriously and, in so doing, we've managed to pull off art, literature, philosophy, technology, science, civilisation itself. It's an extraordinary achievement. But we should be more curious. Why should there be such a thing as reason? And why should the three pounds of grey matter between my ears be any good at grasping it? This didn't need to be the case. But it is.

However clichéd we might find the idea, it's still true: life is a gift. We can't do anything in this world—we can't move a muscle, or even *contemplate* moving a muscle—without relying wholesale on the most extraordinary gifts.

If we imagine that we've pulled ourselves up by our bootstraps in this world, we're like a businessman who boasts of his millions when actually he inherited *billions* from Mum and Dad. He's not a self-made man at all. It's all been given.

Could it be that we are all in that businessman's position? In our best moments, we sense how absolutely fantastic it is to be alive. And in our honest moments, we recognise that to be alive is a gift.

The Giver

So minute by minute, we rely on a thousand givens nested inside a thousand others. In fact, *we* are nested inside these givens. But if every given should be regarded as a gift, then every gift should be traced to its Giver.

Allow me to lead you in a little thought experiment. Bring to mind all the givens of your life: you, your mind, your body, your talents, every material blessing, every experience you've had in your life so far, your culture, your world, the whole harmonious universe with lucky old you thrown into the mix. Try to hold it in your mind. (I know it's tricky, but have a go.) Do you see it all? Picture the cosmos on the computer screen of your mind, perhaps with a little arrow indicating "You are here".

Now move the mouse down to the scroll bar at the bottom of your vision. Press rewind, and don't stop. Watch the whole thing reversing—each gift you enjoy swallowed by its prior source. Go back before this century, and then before this millennium, and then before this civilization... before the trees, and the land, and this planet, and this galaxy. Keep pressing rewind. Now you're back before the material universe, but don't stop rewinding. And you say, "Why, what's the point? The universe is everything, right?" No, it's really not. The universe is given.

If you keep pressing rewind, you'll find the Giver. What would that look like? The Giver behind all the gifts—the being who was there before anything came to be. Traditionally we call him "God". But let's now think: what would *he* look like?

The Bible says that even before the beginning of time, there was an unbreakable life of love. There was a Father forever loving his Son, and filling him with the Holy Spirit (John 17 v 24; John 3 v 34). This is the Christian understanding of God. God is "Trinity": that is, a "unity of three". Don't let the word put you off. What it *describes* is this: as you keep pressing the rewind button—pressing it for all eternity—you get to the point where all you ever see is a Niagara Falls of self-giving love: the Father loving his Son in the life-giving joy of the Holy Spirit. This is what the Bible means by that little word "God".

Back and back and back you go, but you never get before, behind or beyond this overflowing love. It's the original reality and the origin of everything else. Here we find an ocean with no bottom. Unplumbable depths. Unfathomable fullness. Infinite bliss. Here, in the beginning, is the Giver to explain the givens. It's not just that God is a Giver and we are the takers (though that is true); it's that God is beginningless and endless love—Father, Son and Spirit in an eternal and ecstatic give-and-take.

Why do we resonate with giving and receiving? Why do we love Christmas? Is it possible that Christmas, at its best, reflects something of God?

Ultimate Christmas

Think of the ultimate Christmas. It's family and friends united in love and joy. It's celebration and thankfulness. It's giving and receiving. It's playfulness and rest. We'll think in the next chapter of Christmas at its worst, but for now, let's acknowledge the good. Christmas connects us with what's best in life. And if we take the Bible's vision of God seriously, we come to see *why*. According to the Bible, the ultimate reality—God—is a union of giving and receiving! There has always been an unbreakable love, fierce and indivisible—a Father,

Son and Holy Spirit united completely, where giving and receiving is the essence of their life. Jesus, when he was on earth, described it like this:

Father ... you loved me before the creation of the world.
(The Gospel of John, chapter 17, verse 24)

Or consider this way of putting it:

The Father loves the Son and has placed everything in his hands. (John 3 v 35)

When we offer and receive our Christmas gifts, when we dance back and forth with "You shouldn't have!" and "I wanted to!", when we find rest in the loving embrace of another—we are resonating with something very deep and very old. The universe hums with this wonder, and every now and then we hear its tune. Christmas is the faintest reflection of that original love that brought us into being—an original love that we're invited to share.

That's why Christmas *can be* so wonderful. That's why Christmas often *is* so wonderful. But we all know it can go wrong...

2. "YOU SHOULDN'T HAVE"

Two years ago I experienced ten minutes of Christmas hell. Being the generous sort, I decided to share the hell around a bit. Since "misery loves company", I dragged my wife Emma into the pit with me.

We were at my in-laws' place (before you smirk, that's not what made it hell). My wife and I were staying in the spare room. It wasn't the best place to have a argument (not that anywhere is particularly good for it), but this wasn't something we'd planned. So we improvised. We whispered—hiss-pered really—for ten minutes.

The cause of our dispute? A Christmas gift. You're thinking, "How did you manage to fight about a gift?" I agree, it was unspeakably moronic, but I'm not done explaining the true stupidity of this spat. The cause of our Christmas quarrel was a present given to our three-year-old, which she adored. Those were all the ingredients we needed to concoct hell. It was "the most wonderful time of the year", with the woman I love more than anyone on earth, concerning a gift which made a toddler squeal with delight. But once you add Glen Scrivener to the mix, stand back and watch the carnage.

"I Don't Know What Came Over Me"

How were we able to conjure hell out of our heavenly circumstances? I'm still not really sure. All I know is that at the time it felt like a dreaded inevitability, like being sucked into a black hole of empty, needless spite. Flesh soured, blood fizzed, bones heavied. And as my head throbbed hot with the vital aim of winning this argument, another part of my subconscious roused itself: "Are we really doing this? We are, are we? Right, and… Oh no. Please no, you're not going to say that, are you?" Apparently I was! Apparently I was capable of saying all sorts of monstrosities.

Still you're asking yourself, "What on earth could have caused such an eruption?" And no answer seems adequate. Take a large dollop of Christmas expectations, throw in a helping of family traditions, sprinkle liberally with fear, pride, shame and envy, mix thoroughly and bring to the boil. Even so, you're objecting: "How do these ingredients add up to the horror you're describing? What on earth caused it?" But that's exactly the thing: it didn't feel as if anything on earth could cause it. That's why I keep using the hell language.

It took ten minutes before one of us said, "Wait, can we start over?" A Christmas truce was called—a ceasefire. But it was costly. It meant letting go of anger and swallowing our pride. Somehow, though, the cycle was broken and "peace and goodwill towards men" was restored.

In breathless wonder my wife and I looked back at the last ten minutes of gut-churning, soul-sapping horror, and we did what any couple does in this situation. We lied. "Sorry, honey, it wasn't me. I don't know what came over me!" Of course, this wasn't really true. It *was* me. And nothing "came over" me that morning. It all came out of me—out of somewhere very deep and dark. It came out of me, yet it was bigger than me. The words were truly mine, but somehow they had overpowered me. Have you ever felt what I'm describing?

Fire and Fury

Here is some ancient wisdom that, I've found, perfectly captures these situations:

> *The tongue ... is a fire, a world of evil among the parts of the body. It corrupts the whole body, sets the whole course of one's life on fire, and is itself set on fire by hell. (James 3 v 6)*

Those words come from the Bible, and when James, the author here, mentions the tongue, he's not speaking anatomically. He means our words. Words burn. I'm guessing you've experienced this. Perhaps you've been burnt by words. Perhaps you've roasted others. According to the Bible, we are all involved in sparking and in suffering these flames.

Billy Joel once sang, "We didn't start the fire; it was always burning since the world's been turning". James can agree up to a point, but he doesn't let us off the hook completely. Yes, the fire is much bigger and much older than us. But, on the other hand, we each play our own part. Our tongues are *ours* after all. They're a part of who we are. With that in mind, notice all the ways in which the tongue is described: a fire, a world of evil, a corrupting force, a spreading destroyer. That's us. That's *me*. Shocking! Am I really so mixed up in the evil around me? Apparently.

Then notice the end of the sentence: our lives are themselves "set on fire by hell". We dish out the hell even as we are consumed by it. We light the fires and are lit. It comes out of us, and yet is bigger than us. A hell of a problem.

Forsaking the Fountain

There's something maddeningly wrong with the world. On the one hand it's full of wonder and joy, family, food and festivities. Christmas can be genuinely heavenly—a reflection of the love we were made for. But at the very same time, even on the very same day, it can be a hell of a world.

One snapshot of our predicament comes in another part of the Bible—the Old Testament book of Jeremiah. Here God pictures it like this:

My people have committed two sins:
They have forsaken me,
the spring of living water,
and have dug their own [wells],
broken [wells] that cannot hold water.
(Jeremiah 2 v 13)

What is God like? A Fountain. He is the Source of life and satisfaction. He is not a needy Taker but an overflowing Giver, gushing with soul-slaking joy.

What are we like? We are people who crave wholeness and happiness like water in the desert. Instead of receiving that from God, though, we walk past the Giver and take a shovel to dry ground. We are well-diggers, desperate for the life which freely flows from God. Yet we ignore the Giver and try to eke out our existence by ourselves and for ourselves. What do we get for all our labours? A mouthful of mud.

Apply this to our Christmas argument. Emma and I had both turned to our own "broken wells"—faulty sources of life and joy. Our broken wells were things like "being right", "an easy life", and "family approval". With our eyes on these lesser goals, we could only view the other person as an obstacle. And what do you do with obstacles? Cherish them? No, you push them aside if you can.

A Failure to Receive

This is the problem with the world. Instead of give-and-take, we grasp-and-tear. Instead of being filled by the original Giver and pouring out to others, we feel empty by ourselves and try to use others. We identify people as means to our ends or as obstacles in our way. It begins with a failure to receive from God, our true life source. It continues with our desperate attempts to make life work on our own terms. And so we tap into everything and every*one* to give us the significance we crave. And it works. Sort of. For a bit. But not really. Because nothing finite can fill us.

So when those people and those goals fail us as sources of life, we end up mad, miserable and muttering. We end up lashing out at the people we love, resenting them because they're not an unfailing fountain—they're not God. And neither are we. Therefore we'll manage to say the very worst things to the people we say we adore. So we ask the question again, this time with profound disappointment: *What are we like?*

From bedrooms to boardrooms to classrooms to war rooms, all of us are empty well-diggers using others to make ourselves feel full. That's not the whole story, obviously. There is also that lovely gift-giving stuff we thought about last chapter. That bit is also true of us. Genuinely. But it's both. The generosity and the jealousy, the grace and the grasping are all jumbled together. It's quite a cocktail. But then again, that's true of the whole world, wouldn't you say? Breath-taking beauty and jaw-dropping evil.

The world around us and our hearts within us display the same mixture. Which means that I'm a part of the problem with the world. Or at least, a part of me is a part of the problem. Yet this part of me is *really* part of me. Deeply. Stubbornly. It erupts out of me even at the most wonderful time of the year. It's me, and it's beyond me, and it comes through me, and it poisons all that I love. A hell of a problem.

The Arc of the Moral Universe

In an article in 1958, the American civil rights campaigner Martin Luther King used a saying that has since become popular: "Yes, the arc of the moral universe is long, but it bends toward justice". It's the idea that history is heading somewhere and that, in the end, there will be final justice—a righting of wrongs.

It's an attractive idea because we don't want history to be meaningless. We don't want injustice to be forgotten, evil unpunished or goodness lost for ever. We have a sense that this world is a story, and we know how stories are supposed to end: the good guys win, the bad guys get their just deserts, and the truth will out.

But before we clamour for perfect justice, perhaps we should be careful what we wish for. Sometimes the bad guy is me. Sometimes the injustice is mine. What makes me think I'll be on the right side of history?

In many ways I have acted like a spoilt child in God's world, taking his generous gifts and ignoring him. My failure to properly receive God's good gifts is not just foolish, not just destructive—it's a personal insult. When I reject the gift, I reject the Giver. And the God who is love is rightly angered by our loveless and unlovely ways. The God who is the Giver is rightly appalled by our grasping and greed.

Martin Luther King was right—God is bending all things towards justice. As he does so, he brings that justice to bear in our own lives. His judgments begin in this life—he sometimes hands us over to the consequences of our own selfishness. But if we continue on a path that is against God and against the moral arc of his universe, we will find ourselves on the wrong side of his final judgment. We will face a future without any of the good gifts we enjoy or the givens we've taken for granted. That's what the Bible calls hell. It's like all the hellish moments that we've felt along the way, but unshackled and unending.

Yet God does not want this for anyone. Hence Christmas.

Christmas to the Rescue

The last few pages have been, let's face it, a bit of a downer. I wonder what your response has been.

When we hear about the human problem, one natural reaction is to redouble our efforts. We resolve to do better. We pledge to be less hellish in the future. That's not a bad idea, but it can't be the solution. I promise you, I wasn't *trying* to be hellish on that Christmas morning. I was actually trying—*really* trying—to make heaven on earth (my way, of course). Nevertheless, I was swept up in a problem far bigger than me. This is why I need a solution that is, likewise, far bigger than me.

So before we ask what we will do about the human problem, let's ask the more important question. What will *God* do?

If he were a different kind of God, he might simply wash his hands of us, leave us to our hell and start again—perhaps throw his lot in with a promising new start-up planet in the next galaxy along. By rights God should leave us in our pit for ever. And he will, if we insist on rejecting his help.

But that's not God's desire. This God we're talking about loves. This God is a *Giver*. So what does *he* do?

He sees our ingratitude and our world-wrecking selfishness, and he decides on the perfect response. He gives us a gift.

3. "I WANTED TO"

The Bible is the world's all-time best-selling book. Its most famous verse is probably John 3 v 16, sometimes described as "the Bible in a nutshell". Some people go to extraordinary lengths to write even just the verse reference onto pieces of cardboard so that they can hold it up at sporting events. If they're going to be on TV, maybe they write it on their clothing or their bare torso—even in the dead of winter. They tattoo it on body parts or just print it on bumper stickers.

They are desperate for people to follow the reference, dust off an old Bible and look it up. Those who really grasp this verse's significance consider this message such good news that the whole world should sit up and listen.

I completely agree with them. These words are beyond astonishing. Here they are:

For God so loved the world that he gave his one and only Son, that whoever believes in him shall not perish but have eternal life. (John 3 v 16)

This is the great gift, given to an unworthy world.

We're Not Worthy

The world, as we saw last chapter, is not a worthy recipient. For a start, the world *couldn't* earn God's gift. The world has no possessions, no credit, no currency that isn't originally the property of God anyway. We can't really give to God, and we can't really earn from him. Everything already belongs to the one who is, by definition, the Giver. As the Bible puts it:

"Who has ever given to God,
that God should repay them?"
For from him and through him and for him
are all things.
To him be the glory for ever!
                    (Romans 11 v 35-36)

At Christmas we are bombarded with ads that ask, "What do you buy the man who has it all?" Usually the advertiser answers their own question by suggesting *some kind of aftershave*. This seems like a paltry gift, considering the wealth of the man in question. But actually, if he really did own all things, then *nothing* would be an appropriate gift. For a start, you'd have to buy the gift with his money—he owns everything after all. And you'd have to wrap it in his own stash of paper and send the package cash on delivery. Oh, and don't forget, *he already owns the aftershave!* If the man really has it all, then there's nothing you can give him. Likewise, if God is the original and ultimate Giver, then you can't give him anything. You can't reimburse him for his kindness. It's all already his.

So by nature we can't *earn* God's gifts, because we hold no assets of our own. But there's a deeper truth about our unworthiness. Considering the way we've used God's gifts in the past—the way we've ignored the Giver and mistreated his world—we really, *really* don't deserve another gift. Especially not *this* gift. Quite the opposite—we deserve to be left in our pit.

But God loves us. He "*so* loved the world that he gave…"

Do You Love Me?
Sometimes, when I'm feeling particularly insecure, I'll ask my wife, "Do you love me?" It's pathetic,

I know, but not half as pathetic as my follow up question: "But why? Why do you love me?" This is the killer. The poor woman is now in a bind. Anything she says at this point can—and probably will—create panic. Anything.

If, for instance, she says, "I love you because you provide for the family," my blood pressure will shoot up. You see, I might lose my job. Would I then lose her love?

If she says, "I love you because of your chiselled good looks," this too is problematic. For a start, it's not true. The only chiselled part of me is a nose that looks as if it's been hewn from concrete with a jackhammer. But even if I *did* possess boy-band good looks, looks fade (or, in my case, decompose like roadkill). They are an unstable foundation for love. If you are loved because of your looks, you will be anxious.

Even if my wife tells me that she loves me for my *inner* beauty—my kindness, or something—this is not ultimately comforting. For a start, I know that often I'm not kind. And, more than this, who knows what will happen in the future? I might get dementia and leave this earth swearing my head off in a nursing home. I hope that the love of my family is stronger than my unlovely behaviour. If you want a love that lasts, you will need a love that goes beyond what you deserve.

The correct answer to the question "Emma, why do you love me?" is "Glen, I love you because I love you because I love you because I always will. Now quit being so needy." This is the love we must have: love that is not based on *our* character but on the character of the lover. Wonderfully, that's what we have with God. He loves us not because of what we're like. God loves us because of what he's like.

God does not love the worthy. He loves those who don't deserve it. He loves those who can't deserve it. If he loved only the worthy, then we'd be in trouble. If the answer to the question "Why does God love me?" began with "Because I...", an unbearable weight would fall on our shoulders. The question would become "Have I done it enough? Am I worthy enough? Do I qualify?" But wonderfully, God's love is not conditional on what we're like. It's simply based on who he is.

What Is He Like?

God is a Giver—and what does he give? John 3 v 16 goes on to tell us that, incredibly, he gives his "one and only Son"—his heart and soul, his pride and joy. The Father has for ever filled his Son with his Spirit. The Father has for ever cherished and adored the apple of his eye. The Father has, as we've already seen, placed everything in the hands of his Son (John 3 v 35). The Son is the Prince of heaven, the Co-creator of the world, the Heir of the cosmos… and it is *he* who is given to us. On that first Christmas in Bethlehem, the Son of God entered into creation as a human baby—Jesus. As one old carol proclaims…

> *Lo, within the manger lies*
> *He who built the starry skies.*

If this isn't astonishing enough, look at the gift tag around his ankle: "From: *God*. To: *You*." This baby is a gift not just to the world in general but to you in particular.

And Jesus is the ultimate gift because in giving us his Son, the Father is giving us himself. We have already thought about how the best presents are the ones we put ourselves into. This is true of the ultimate present: God is offering himself to the world in this most personal of gifts.

The God who gave you blue skies and sparkling seas, air to breathe and eyes to see—the God who gave you a mind, music, mercy upon mercy and miracle upon miracle—now gives you a gift beyond calculation. Having given you a world, having given you *you*, he now gives you himself. Because this is how love operates. Love gives, whatever the cost.

Christmas was just the beginning.

The Gift of His Life

One of the names of Jesus is "Immanuel". It's a Hebrew word meaning "God with us". If you read the Gospels—the biographies of Jesus' life—you are reading eyewitness accounts of God walking the earth. Here is the Son of the Father, who became our brother. He has come to live life *with* us, in solidarity with us, as one of us.

And what does that look like? It looks like towering authority and stooping love. Blistering rebuke to the holier-than-thou and tender mercy to the down-and-outs. Jesus miraculously produces wine for a wedding and then, in the same chapter, drives out religious hypocrites from the temple (John 2). He sleeps through a hurricane, and then flattens it with a word. He shows up late to the funeral of a beloved friend, cries so much that he out-mourns every guest, and then raises the dead man to life. He claims to be God without hesitation, and then serves beneath all human dignity.

Day after day, without exception, Jesus lived his life with perfect peace and love. Instead of dishing out hellish behaviour, he absorbed it. Instead of using people to fill himself up, he poured himself out to satisfy others. He always trusted and obeyed his Father, the Fountain of life. He was always on the right side of justice.

Here was life as it's meant to be lived, and he lived it for you.

The Gift of His Death

At Christmas Jesus stooped down to our humanity, but throughout his life he kept on stooping—all the way to his death on a cross. In order to meet us in the depths of our hellish predicament, Jesus set out resolutely for Jerusalem, where he knew he would meet his fate. While many tried to talk him out of it, no one could. His followers were left bewildered by a man who showed the most extraordinary combination of motives: a God-complex and a death-wish.

Why was Jesus so determined to die? Because he loves. Love says, "Your plight will be my plight. Your struggles will be my struggles. Your debts will be my debts." When Jesus saw us in the pit of our own making, he resolved to love us. On the cross he was paying our debts, taking our judgment, suffering our hell. He perished so that we might "not perish" (John 3 v 16).

This was the death we should have died, and it was offered for you.

The Gift of His Resurrection

We all sometimes wonder what's on the other side of death. Many answer, "We'll never know. No one has come back to tell us." In the resurrection, Jesus begs to differ. He died our death on the cross and then, on Easter Sunday—to the utter astonishment of his friends—he rose up to new life.

His death-defeating resurrection was not just a one-off, freak occurrence. Jesus was pioneering a new reality—one which we are invited to share in: "Because I live, you also will live," he said (John 14 v 19). Jesus is like a needle that pierces through the black shroud of death and emerges out the other side. If we are connected to Jesus by trusting in him, we are the thread. The new life, hope and grave-conquering joy of Jesus can be ours. We can receive "eternal life" (John 3 v 16).

This is the hope we need for the future, and it is offered for you.

The Gift of Himself

But that's not even the best bit.

What is the best bit about the gift of Jesus? Well, suppose I were to ask someone, "What's the best thing you get out of your marriage?" Hopefully they wouldn't say "money", or "tax-breaks" or "a green card". Hopefully they'd say, "The best thing I get out of my marriage is my spouse." Likewise, the greatest thing we are offered by Jesus is not forgiveness or joy or feelings of purpose, or even eternal life. The greatest thing we are offered by Jesus is Jesus himself. He is the gift of the Father: "God so loved the world that he *gave his one and only Son*" (John 3 v 16).

This isn't just something that happened way back in history. Jesus offers to be with us today. By his Spirit, Jesus takes up personal residence in the lives of those who trust him—to be with us for ever, through all life's twists and turns. Like a bride or groom in the wedding service, Jesus says, "All that I am I give to you. All that I have I share with you."

There's nothing greater he could give us, and so he gives us himself.

Jesus is the gift of God—the gift that keeps on giving.

For God so loved the world that he gave his one and only Son, that whoever believes in him shall not perish but have eternal life.

The Christmas Child is the gift above all gifts.

So the question is, what will we do with it?

5. "THANK YOU!"

"Alfie! Look! What's this?"

"Pwesent!!"

"Who's it for?"

"Me!"

"Who's it from?"

"Unkoo Paul."

"What do you say?"

"Fank you!"

"How do you like it? Alfie? … Alfie??"

[A wide-eyed Alfie is engrossed for the rest of the afternoon.]

Even little kids know what to do with a gift. They acknowledge the giver, they receive the gift, they say thank you, and they enjoy it.

If I give Alfie a present, I don't want him to spend the afternoon tugging at my trouser leg and mouthing continual thanks. "Enough already," I'll say. "Go and have fun!" It's true that you don't appreciate the gift if you never say thank you. It's also true that you don't appreciate the gift if you *only* say thank you. One of the chief ways Alfie can honour me, the giver, is if he spends the next three hours absorbed in his Batman Lego. Better yet, we can play with it together.

We give gifts not for what we get back. We give them freely, hoping the recipient will use and enjoy them. It's the same with God. He has given us his Son, and he wants us to respond. That means four things.

Acknowledge the Giver

In Christmas services all over the world, the Old Testament prophet Isaiah is quoted. He spoke 700 years before the first Christmas, predicting the time when the "Mighty God" would come to his people (Isaiah 9 v 6). But this "Mighty God" would not come in thunder and dread. He would come purely as a gift.

To us a child is born,
to us a son is given. (Isaiah 9 v 6)

In those two little words, "to us", you have the heart of God. What is he like? He's a Fountain of life, a Giver without beginning or end. He entered a world that has proved itself thoroughly untrustworthy. Yet still he came. Still he gave himself.

Have you let Christmas change your view of God? As you see him offering himself to you, do you acknowledge the kind of God that he is—that he is a Giver? Does he seem like the kind of God who can be trusted?

Receive the Gift

What do you do with a gift? You don't leave it underneath the Christmas tree. You receive it. As it says in John, the biography of Jesus that we've been considering…

To all who did receive [Jesus], to those who
believed in his name, he gave the right to
become children of God. (John 1 v 12)

"Receiving Jesus" and "believing in him" are not two different things. They are two descriptions of the same reality. And that's very helpful because it gives us another way of understanding "believing".

"Believing" is not about agreeing with a bunch of facts. It's not like believing that light takes eight minutes to reach the earth from the sun. To believe in Jesus is personal. It means to receive him, to take him into your life, to accept him, to embrace him. Believing is receiving.

And to receive Jesus is to be received into God's family—to become a child of God. If you accept Jesus, then his Father becomes your Father, his Spirit becomes your Spirit, his brothers and sisters in the church become your brothers and sisters in the church. What a give-and-take! As we receive, so we are received—drawn into bonds of unbreakable love.

The gift of Christ is not like an Amazon gift card. It is not an impersonal present to be spent on your own wish list! It is a personal union. The Lord of all comes into your life and you, in turn, come into his. With this ultimate Christmas gift, you are not given a *thing*; you are given a person. And through him—through Jesus—you are invited into a family of love. For ever.

Will you embrace this gift or leave it unopened? Throughout this book you've seen what's on offer. All that's left to do is receive it—to receive *him*.

And if we receive him, we'll know what to say next…

Say Thank You

If life is a gift, then the secret to a life well lived is gratitude. The Bible constantly urges Jesus' followers to be "overflowing with thankfulness" (Colossians 2 v 7, for example). We have so many reasons to be grateful. Amid our many trials and sorrows—and there are many—we are on the receiving end of miraculous blessings. And when we see the ultimate gift of Jesus, given with every drop of his blood, how can we doubt the generosity of God? How can we not say a hearty thank you?!

In doing so, we begin to reverse our inborn ingratitude and our well-digging ways. When we naturally feel proud or angry or jealous or aggrieved or deserving or bitter—hellish emotions that so readily bubble to the surface of our lives—the most effective antidote is a healthy dose of gratitude. Each day I remind myself, "In all my pathetic, well-digging ways, there is a Fountain of life who overflows with everything I'm seeking." Therefore, I return to the source to say "thank you."

And finally...

Enjoy

God gives us his gift as uncles give Batman Lego. He wants us to run along and enjoy it—to enjoy his own life of overflowing generosity. The life of Father, Son and Spirit—ecstatic giving and warm receiving—is the life that birthed all other life. It's the source of all creation. Now Jesus has come to give us this life. Here is good news: we don't need to live the empty life of draining others. Now we get to live the full life of pouring ourselves out.

That might sound like bad news: giving up grasping and committing to generosity. But really, it's good news. We can give up on the emptiness of greed and start on the ecstatic life of self-giving love. In our better moments we know the wisdom of this. We know that grasping is wrong and generosity is right—Christmas teaches us that much.

Well then, with Jesus, each day we are invited to live out a kind of Christmas-morning joy. Having received Jesus, we can now, from his fullness, give to a needy world. This is the movement that conquers hell and, on that day in the future when Christ comes again, will establish heaven on earth for ever. It's the gift God has given us. Enjoy!

And You?
If receiving this gift is something that you want to do, let me leave you with a little prayer. It's actually the final verse of a famous carol: "O Little Town

of Bethlehem". I think these eight lines summarise all we've been thinking about. Why not pray it for yourself? You could even personalise the words, turning "us" into "me" and "we" into "I".

Allow these words to be your words and, this Christmas, receive the ultimate gift:

> *O holy Child of Bethlehem,*
> *Descend to us, we pray.*
> *Cast out our sin and enter in,*
> *Be born to us today.*
> *We hear the Christmas angels*
> *The great glad tidings tell;*
> *O come to us, abide with us,*
> *Our Lord Immanuel.*

Read the book? Now watch the film...

We've created a short film called *Let Me Go There*, which brings to life some of the themes we explore in this book.

To watch it, visit **letmegothere.info**

The film is inspired by my favourite Christmas poem, called *The Coming* by R.S. Thomas, and in particular its last line: "Let me go there". It's an imagined request from the Son of God to his Father, spoken before that first Christmas. "Let me go there" is Jesus Christ volunteering for his mission, despite knowing what awaited him: in the words of Thomas's poem, a scorched land, a serpent and a bare tree with "crossed boughs".

In short, the Son knew that the crib would lead to the cross. And still he wanted to come as God's gift to the world.

The gift of Christmas is the gift of the Father sending the Son—his very pride and joy. It's the gift of the Son volunteering to come, no matter what it costs. It's a gift as precious today as when it was first given. It's a gift for you.

"The Father has sent his Son to be the Saviour of the world." (1 John 4 v 14)

thegoodbook
COMPANY

Thanks for reading this book. We hope you enjoyed it, and found it helpful.

Most people want to find answers to the big questions of life: Who are we? Why are we here? How should we live? But for many valid reasons we are often unable to find the time or the right space to think positively and carefully about them.

Perhaps you have questions that you need an answer for. Perhaps you have met Christians who have seemed unsympathetic or incomprehensible. Or maybe you are someone who has grown up believing, but need help to make things a little clearer.

At The Good Book Company, we're passionate about producing materials that help people of all ages and stages understand the heart of the Christian message, which is found in the pages of the Bible.

Whoever you are, and wherever you are at when it comes to these big questions, we hope we can help. As a publisher we want to help you look at the good book that is the Bible because we're convinced that as we meet the person who stands at its heart—Jesus Christ—we find the clearest answers to our biggest questions.

Visit our website to discover the range of books, videos and other resources we produce, or visit our partner site www.christianityexplored.org for a clear explanation of who Jesus is and why he came.

Thanks again for reading,

Your friends at The Good Book Company

thegoodbook.com | thegoodbook.co.uk
thegoodbook.com.au | thegoodbook.co.nz | thegoodbook.co.in

WWW.CHRISTIANITYEXPLORED.ORG

Our partner site is a great place to explore the Christian faith, with powerful testimonies and answers to difficult questions.